THE COWBOY
AN AMERICAN LEGEND

A WESTERN PICTORIAL HISTORY
by
Phyllis Zauner

ZANEL PUBLICATIONS
P. O. Box 1387
Sonoma, CA 95476

Front Cover Picture
Courtesy of Frontier Times Museum
Bandera,Texas

ZANEL publications:

California Gold, Story of the Rush to Riches
Carson City, Capital of Nevada
Lake Tahoe, The Way It Was Then and Now
Sacramento and the California Delta
San Francisco, The Way It Was Then and Now
The Cowboy, An American Legend
Those Legendary Men of the Wild West
Those Spirited Women of the Early West
Virginia City, Its History ... Its Ghosts

It was an era when a man's word was more binding than a written contract, and when personal industry and integrity were held in higher esteem than shrewdness.

– The Author

Tall in the Saddle

The American cowboy is known around the world. His image has been permanently fixed by John Wayne (whose cowboy is stubbornly fair but a terror when wronged), by Waylon Jennings (who sings of the shy cowboy, awkward around women), by artists like Russell and Remington (both of whom rode with cowboys), and by writer Louis L'Amour, who may know more about the frontier cowboy than any other western historian.

The cowboy of fact may have been slightly less romantic than the legend portrayed in movie, song and paint. There was certainly no romance in getting up at four in the morning, eating dust behind a trail herd, swimming muddy rivers, nor in doctoring screw worms, pulling stupid cows from bog holes, sweating in the 110° heat of Arizona or freezing at minus-40° in Montana.

Still, there is the seed of truth in the legend. Myth and reality did converge. The cowboy of the 1870s was awkward around women — because he never saw one. By one account, "a lonesome young cowboy would travel miles just to sit on a porch for an hour or two and watch some homesteader's red-faced daughter rock her chair and scratch her elbows — and not a smack or a hug."

And while the average old-time cowhand may not exactly have fit the picture of a dashing, two-gun hombre riding at a sweeping gallop uphill over rough trails for hours, his horse's eye bulging with the joy of speed, still he sometimes did ride hard and dangerously on the trail and in roundup. And though he was no lawless ruffian, he did fancy carrying a Colt. In truth, it was used mostly on rattlesnakes.

The time of the legendary cowboy and the trail drives lasted a bare generation, from the end of the Civil War (when the first railroads into Kansas opened eastern beef markets), until the mid-1880s, when barbed wire put an end to the old freewheeling ways.

The numbers of cowboys who rode the trails north were no more than 40,000. Yet those bare statistics cannot dim the riveting appeal they generated, in their own time and forever afterward.

His was a job it would be hard to sell. His narrow-toed boots were caked with dirt and cow dung. He wore a black, dirt-splattered Stetson, spurs and chaps. His face was burnt bright red from the scorching sun. His lips and teeth were smeared with chewing tobacco. One old cowhand described his breed as "noisy fellers with bow legs and brass stomachs that rides horses and hates any kind of work they can't do on one."

But he was his own man — a weather-worn frontiersman in a country that belonged to God. He was a cowboy, and he never aspired to any other calling.

The early cowboys were not just cattle herders, they were mounted herdsmen, and that distinction was of profound importance to them and to the development of the personal characteristics that began to shape the cowboy mystique. Shy, self-conscious young men suddenly gained poise and confidence in the saddle. Work that, if done on foot, would have been considered banal, downright demeaning, became a proud occupation when carried out on horseback.

Other states were made or born,
Texas grew from hide and horn.
...Berta Hart Nance

The cowboy sprang into existence in Texas in the 1850s, when some enterprising pioneers took a notion there might be money to be made by catching the free-roaming, half-wild longhorns that were everywhere, and bringing them to market in the East.

If it weren't for the longhorns, the cowboy might never have been. Nor those epic trail drives, and the soulful ballads cowboys sang to soothe ornery cows on night watch along the old Chisholm trail.

Brought to Mexico by early Spanish explorers, longhorns eventually drifted north into Texas where they multiplied with astounding virility. These were the wild herds that in time became the basis of the American cattle kingdom.

The Texas longhorn was something amazing to see — and to fear. Lanky and swaybacked, it could weigh a ton, with a horn spread of six feet tip-to-tip (the record was eight feet).

The longhorn bull was one of the nastiest brutes in creation, an animal well adapted to living in the wild. Entire herds hid in dense thorny thickets, and would attack with daring ferocity, even charging entire military regiments. Any person afoot on the open range was a mighty fool indeed. Only a horse could carry him to safety — if he was lucky.

American settlers know about cattle, of course. But that knowledge meant little in Texas. None who came ever had handled such large numbers of cattle, nor handled them on horseback.

Vaquero

However, their Spanish neighbors — a singular breed of professional horsemen calling themselves vaqueros, had been doing precisely that for centuries. From them, the Texan cowboy learned how to drive a pony through milling seas of cattle, cutting out his ranchero's stock from that of his neighbors. He learned how to throw a loop of braided rawhide rope and bring the animal to a stop by taking quick turns of the lariat around the saddle horn. The vaquero showed him how to ride up behind a running steer, grab its tail and flip the beast hind-over-horn, stunning it.

The Texas cowboy even borrowed Mexican names. Vaquero became buckaroo. Rancho was ranch. The leather pants Mexicans called chaparreras became chaps. La reata was anglicized to lariat. Spanish for "rough horse," bronco caballo, was shortened to bronc.

As he watched and adapted vaquero customs and techniques, inventing others for himself, he discovered he had invented a job that had not existed previously.

He was a cowboy.

The Long Longhorn Trail

To the cowboy of the Old West, nothing was more challenging — or miserable — than the unique and short-lived phenomenon called the Long Drive. It was the grandest, most grueling adventure that cowboy life offered: a 1,200-mile trek that took three months of dust, thirst, blisters, cold and danger to complete — for which the man received $25 to $30 a month. It was a hard way to earn a hundred dollars.

Some idea of just how perilous this experience could be is revealed in a day-by-day account kept by a cowhand named Baylis Fletcher on his first trail drive moving 2,500 head of cattle from Corpus Christi to Dodge, on the old Chisholm Trail.

Trouble started the second day out, Fletcher reports. While guiding the herd through a small town, the cattle were spooked by an old woman flapping her sunbonnet to shoosh them away from her roses. The longhorns took her advice seriously and scattered all over the village. It was hours before they could be regrouped.

A few nights later, the herd was spooked by rustlers. The steers, already nervous, took off in a rumbling stampede. The trail boss's cry, "All hands and the cook!" sent every man in camp out on a frantic night ride. But next morning a hundred steers were still missing.

Once a herd had broken, it was likely to go again and again. One night the heavens opened up, said Fletcher, and dropped hailstones as big as quail eggs, pelting the men and again scattering the herd.

Occasionally the mass of animals would take off for no reason at all, giving the hands another grim night in the saddle.

NO TRAIL TOO ROUGH OR TOO LONG

A trail drive might be directed by the owner himself, but was more likely turned over to a drover with trail experience, since the owner had other responsibilities at home and couldn't be gone that long. The number of cattle varied with the wealth and wisdom of the owner, but was likely to be 2,000 to 3,000 steers, managed by eight to twelve cowboys under the direction of a trail boss, who commanded $125 a month — a princely sum at the time. The cowhands respected him and called him Mister.

The first work for the cowboy who had signed to go "up trail" was road-branding. Since a herd might include cattle of several brands from different owners or from different ranches of the same owner, a common brand — the road brand — was needed. Driving cattle through a chute and pressing the road brand on each was hard work, but anticipations of the drive hurried the job.

Owner's Brand   Trail Brand

Then one early morning, the drive got under way. Cattle were assembled, the wrangler got his remuda of horses under control, and the cowboys set out on the most grueling adventure that cowboy life offered — the Long Drive.

Every man knew the risks, and knew that on the trail he was considered less valuable than the cows he drove. Yet they went eagerly, many no more than boys, testing themselves against the unknown. They would be paid barely more than the price of a new hat and a fancy pair of boots. But there was also the comradeship of the trail, the epic sight of rivers of cattle on the move, and perhaps the proud awareness of being part of something heroic.

The Trail Boss

9

A herd didn't move in one long thin column, but rather in a sort of elongated wedge. Cattle, like people, had different personalities. Immediately upon hitting the trail, the most aggressive animal took the lead and held it throughout the drive. The rest of the herd ballooned out behind, five or six cows wide, and they too generally stayed in their beginning position for the rest of the trail.

Men were positioned at key points in relation to the herd, one on each side of the column. The trail boss rode ahead, to scout for water and pasture, and so did the chuck wagon.

A few hundred feet behind came the outfit's two most experienced men, the point men. It was their job to keep the cattle moving in the right direction. Farther down the line rode the swing men, and at another interval the two flank men, keeping the herd pressed into line. Drag men brought up the rear — worst job in the outfit. Breathing dust through bandanas, they harassed lame or lazy cattle and weak yearlings that fell behind, making them keep up. They ate dust all day, crunched it between their teeth, wiped it out of their eyes. Cowboys said that drag was the best place to learn cuss words.

Off to the side of the column rode the wrangler with his remuda of horses. He moved them along by day, kept an eye on them at night, rounded them up in the morning. The little cow ponies could live on minimum water and range grass. But they couldn't take the hard pace of riding under saddle for more than three or four hours every two days. So the wrangler was likely to have 150 or more horses under his command.

The cowboy's lot was often bitterly hard, with prodigious handouts of misery. Yet tribulations were part of the game, privations were endured without complaint. Acceptance of his lot characterized every cowboy, as can be seen in the entries along the trail in the journal kept by trail driver George Duffield in July 1866.

"Upset our wagon in River & lost Many of our cooking utencils ..was on my Horse the whole night & it raining hard...Lost my Knife...There was one of our party Drowned to day (Mr. Carr) & Several narrow escapes & I among...Many Men in trouble. Horses all give out & Men refused to do anything...Awful night...not having had a bite to eat for 60 hours...Tired...Indians very troublesome...Oh! what a night — Thunder Lightning & rain... we followed our Beeves all night as they wandered about...We Hauled cattle out of the Mud with oxen half the day...Dark days are these to me. Nothing but Bread & Coffee. Hands all Growling & Swearing — everything wet & cold...sick & discouraged. Have not got the Blues but am in Hel of a fix...My back is Blistered badly...I had a sick headache bad...all our letters have been sent to the dead letter office...Flies was worse than I ever saw them...weather very Hot...Indians saucy...one man down with Boils & one with Ague...Found a Human skeleton on the Prairie to day."

Since cattle were sold by weight, speed was never the object of a drive. A leisurely pace allowed the cattle to get plenty of food and rest.

But for the first couple of days, the trail boss liked to quicken the pace to get the cattle moved away from home as soon as possible. Confused and disoriented, the cattle were inclined to feel homesick, and would just as soon give up travel and get back to the old familiar range. The trail boss's aim was to get them "herd broke" and see to it they got so tired they'd lie down at night and forget home.

A Rest on the Drive

Each day's drive followed a set routine.

During the early morning the cattle drifted northward a couple of miles, grazing as they went. Once thrown onto the trail, they'd cover another four or five miles by noon. Then the trail boss would gallop ahead and find a good noonday pasture where no other outfit had already stopped. The point men would watch until they saw him ride a circle and stop broadside of the herd, his horse's head indicating the direction for the cattle to turn.

During the noon stop the cattle rested or grazed while the men ate in shifts so that at least two riders were always keeping watch over the cattle. An hour later the herd would be back on trail.

Passing through Indian Territory, the afternoons passed almost hypnotically, the prairie unfolding before the riders in a slow, majestic panorama. Sometimes Indians would appear, demanding a toll for driving through their lands. The trail boss would raise his two arms high, in the shape of cattle horns, indicating that they could cut out one animal as payment.

When the sun began to sink in the West, the men tending the herd would carefully and gradually work the cattle into a more compact space and urge them toward some open, level ground selected for the bedground. If the herd had been well grazed and watered during the day, they'd stop and gradually a few would lie down in their contented cud-chewing.

Bedding the cattle down was a scientific job requiring that the herd not be crowded too close, nor yet allowed to scatter over too much territory. With patience, the cowboy would "ride 'em down," urging the point and drag cattle closer together. Unless disturbed by some unusual noise, the cattle would lie thus for three or four hours without moving. Then, as of one accord, they'd all get onto their feet, mill about a few minutes, then lie down again, this time on their other side. Thus, the herd had to be bedded loose enough to give each animal room to rise and turn over, but not so loose that the herd would scatter and take too much of the cowboy's time as the night herders rode around it.

Every man in camp had night herding duty (except the cook and wrangler). Two at a time, they rode in opposite directions, circling the herd. Riding forty feet from the herd so as not to disturb them, they sang as they rode. If all went well, the singing soothed the cattle and nothing happened until the man was relieved by the next guard. It was long, lonesome duty.

The next guard seldom had to be awakened. Sleeping with his ear to the ground, he could hear the rider coming off herd when still a long distance away, and by the time he reached camp the new guard was ready to take his place.

One of the serious hazards for the trail drive headed north was the geographical inconvenience that rivers flowed east-west and had to be crossed by anyone traveling north.

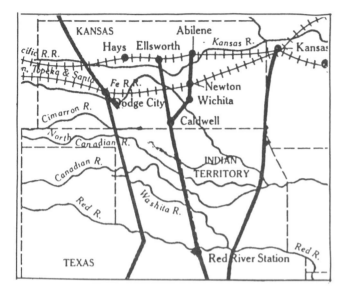

Crossing a herd over a flooded stream, muddy and running with a swift current, was a situation escaped only by the trail drivers of late summer.

The lead cattle instinctively feared such water, and the point riders had hard work urging them on. Sometimes riders would force their own horses into the stream to convince the cattle there was no danger. Once the cattle were out to their swimming depth, they usually went on to the opposite bank and the rest of the herd followed.

But if the river was high and turbulent — "big swimming" it was called — or if the sun was in their eyes and they couldn't see the opposite bank, or if a piece of driftwood struck against a steer, the cattle would mill in a panic-stricken circle, becoming a confused struggling mass as other cattle followed and crowded in. Then came crucial labors for the trail men. Cattle on the bank had to be held back, and a point rider had to force his mount into the middle of the frightened mass, break up the mill and force some of the cattle to lead off toward the far shore. It was a dangerous job. The cowboy sometimes had to desert his horse and crawl over the backs of the cattle to get them turned. Then he'd slip back, to be ferried over by hanging to the tail of some animal.

A trail boss had to be quick-witted. When George Arnett rode ahead of the herd to inspect a river near the Kansas border, he discovered it was fouled from an enormous deposit of alkali that was certain to kill the cattle if they drank it. Yet the day's drive had been dry, and he knew they'd be desperate to drink while fording the river.

He could think of only one solution. Stampede the herd.

The men kept the cattle under tight control right up to the river bank, then on a signal from Arnett they rattled their ponchos and rain slickers wildly to spook the herd. The cows took off in total disarray, right through the river and out the other side. Once they realized they had missed an opportunity to drink, they tried to turn back, thus giving the riders a rough night as well as part of the next day, persuading them to move along.

Crossing a river with a herd of wild longhorns, under any circumstances, took courage, and no higher compliment could be paid a man than to say of him, "He'd do to ride the river with."

Legendary cowboy Charles Siringo reported that when he reached the Salt Fork near the Kansas line he found "bank full and still rising...at least half a mile to the opposite side and driftwood coming down at a terrible rate." Still, the attempt had to be made. "The old lead steers went right into the foaming water, and of course the balance followed." But an easy crossing was not to be his. The horse of one of the point riders sank, and the whole herd turned back in terrible confusion.

There were other hazards in a river crossing — treacherous banks, undercurrents, suck holes. But the worst was quicksand. Once an animal started to sink, it might go down inch by inch for a day until its nose finally went under. Usually, though, the cowboys could rescue it by a difficult and risky procedure. Because the cow's legs stuck like anchors in the quicksand, cowhands would burrow around each leg, double it at the knee and tie it. Thus trussed, the animal could be pulled out by roping its horns to four or five horses.

It was a rare river crossing that went smoothly.

Finally back on the trail, the herd would be paced until sunset, "bedding time." The boss slowly waved his hat in a circle over his head to signal the men along the line, and the herd was moved off trail to the bedground. The first of the four watches of the night took its turn, and the other men gathered about the cook's campfire to eat generously of a hot supper.

As each of the night herders rode his arc of the circle around the resting herd, the slow, deep-sounded notes of old songs could be heard — sweet songs like "When You and I Were Young, Maggie," songs that permitted a soothing prolongation of each note to quiet the cattle and help keep the herder awake.

COWBOY LULLABIES

Most cowboy ballads were sung without words by night herders to quiet stampede-prone cattle. Any song would do as long as it had a lonesome sound that could travel as slow as a walking horse. Nightherding songs were always a croon.

A trail song was different. Composed impromptu, it told a doleful tale of the miseries of cowboy life and had endless verses added on as each cowboy contributed a few new troubles. One that became a standard favorite was "The Old Chisholm Trail."

I'm up in the mornin' afore daylight
And afore I sleep the moon shines bright.
Come a ki-yi-yippe yay...

No chaps and no slicker and it's pouring down rain
And I swear, by God, that I'll never ride again.
Come a ki-yi-yippe yay...

I went to the boss to draw my roll.
He had it figured out I was nine dollars in the hole.
Come a ki-yi-yippe yay...

I'll sell my horse and I'll sell my saddle,
You can go to hell with your longhorn cattle.
Come a ki-yi-yippe yay...

There was no shortage of cattle in Texas. They were, in fact, so plentiful as to be nearly worthless. Until the 1850s the main commercial value of this abundance was to haul the cattle off to the local hide-and-tallow factory to be butchered. Hides were cured, the tallow made soap and candles.

There was a real market for beef in the East. But between the Lone Star State and the butcher shops of New York lay 1,200 miles of inhospitable territory...a hopelessly long way to drive cattle.

Still, wherever the glitter of gold can be seen, there are men willing to defy obstacles.

When the California gold rush of 1849 brought a flood of prospectors there to seek their fortune, a desperate demand for beef developed. Lucky miners were willing to pay any price for a steak. And the Texans, cattle-rich and money-poor, suddenly saw a vision of a bonanza all their own.

The journey from Texas to Sacramento was long, filled with unspeakable hardships. A few cowboys made the trip and some cashed in. Big. But those who tried also set records for endurance. Herds had to cross vast stretches of desert, leaving behind a trail of dead cattle that became mounds of bleached bones stretching for miles.

More bizarre was the adventure of a couple of cowmen named Malone and Pointing, who saw their financial bonanza in herding 800 head of cattle to New York. They managed to get them to Muncie, Indiana for shipping on trains equipped with stock cars. Then the animals were unloaded in New York City, and herded downtown along Third Avenue, to a market on 24th Street.

New Yorkers had never seen anything like the Texas longhorn, and the Texas longhorns had never seen anything like New York city life. They stampeded, overflowed sidewalks and sent pedestrians scurrying for cover. In total panic, people slipped and slithered through manure-filled streets. Grown men ran for their lives, women grabbed kids and pulled them to safety.

Newspapers later reported that the beef was "a little tough," but the steers brought the cowmen $80 a head — a high price for the time.

The cowboy's working partner was a Plains mongrel called the Cow Pony, half-wild and totally ornery, roaming free in large numbers. Living on survival rations on open range grass, they never grew beyond 900 pounds.

Stampede!

As hectic as a river crossing could be, nothing compared to a stampede for sheer terror. And nothing could happen so suddenly. "Boys, the cattle's runnin'!" brought the punchers back from dreamland in a hurry.

Nights of lightning and rain seemed to tighten the cattle's nerves and cause the most trouble. But some things that startled them into running were ordinary, even trifling. A tumbleweed, a jackrabbit, the flare of a match could set them off. On one drive, a shred of tobacco from a cowboy's pouch lodged in a steer's eye, starting a raging charge that resulted in the loss of 400 cows.

We were crossing the Little Missouri once a few miles above Alzada [Montana]. . . . The steers were on water, some drinking, some laying down resting and pretty well scattered along the river. One of the steers was rubbing himself on an old post oak of which there were quite a lot along there. The top was dead and it fell off on top of him. What a stampede! They all went out of there like a flash, and got 10 miles before we could get them checked. Some of the boys on herd said they didn't know what happened, but thought the world was coming to an end.

Ordinarily when a cow rose from the ground, it got into a praying attitude on its knees and rose on its hind feet. But when scared, it jumped straight into the air and landed on all four feet. It was amazing how many cattle could rise simultaneously and be gone, As one cowhand said, "They jes' buy a through ticket to hell-and-gone, and try to ketch the first train." Oddly, they uttered no sound at all. A trail hand sleeping would suddenly be aware of a deep rumbling, and know that the cattle were off. Touched off by something as trivial as the moon rising from the back of a mesa, the great assembly would leap up as if raised by a keg of gunpowder. Away they'd go in a mad, blind frenzy. They saw nothing, they heeded nothing, they stopped at nothing.

When cattle stampeded, they often ran until exhausted. In a four-mile run on a hot night, a beef could lose up to 50 pounds, which was murder on the rancher's profits. It was a lot worse for the cowboy.

A poor cowboy or two, insignificant mites on insignificant ponies, raced ahead of that uncontrollable tidal wave of wild-eyed, stark-mad longhorns. Riding at breakneck speed through the night to check a stampede was the most dangerous part of a perilous job. In country pocked with prairie-dog holes, his life depended on the sure-footedness of his horse. A spill meant certain death, with both horse and rider thrown into the path of the oncoming herd. The punchers dashing ahead in front of them could only hope, by the flashes of their six-guns or any other expedient, to gradually turn them and set them into a "mill," where, in time, they would race themselves to exhaustion going round and round and round and getting nowhere. All this at full speed, generally over treacherous ground, in the black of night, and possibly in a thunderstorm.

With the stampede at last under control, it was time for a hasty inventory. The sudden swerve of the cattle might have crushed to death a cowboy and his horse. Cattle sometimes rushed over a bluff or off a steep river bank, killing some in the pile-up. Some might be gored by the long horns of those they brushed against. If the riders failed to check the herd and hold it in a mass, it might become widely scattered, demanding a delay of days while the remnants were gathered.

Controlling a Stampede
(From *Prose and Poetry of the Livestock Industry*)

BY COLONEL CHARLES GOODNIGHT, famous Texas pioneer and cattleman

The task of the men was to gain control of the herd and gradually turn the cattle until they were moving in a wide circle. Then, although they might break each other's horns off and crush one another badly, the great danger was past. The well trained night horse needed little guidance and knew that if the herd came his way, all he had to do was to lead. The speed of the herd was terrific, but the position at the head of the stampede was what the trail man desired, for he was in the position to start the herd turning.

In the excitement of a stampede a man was not himself and his horse was not the horse of yesterday. Man and horse were one and the combination accomplished feats that would be utterly impossible under ordinary circumstances. Trained men would be generally found near the *point* at both sides of the herd. When the man on one side saw the herd bending his way, he would fall back and if the work was well done on the other side of the herd, the stampede would gradually come to an end; the strain was removed, the cowboys were the happiest men on earth, and their shouts and laughter could be heard for miles over the prairie. . . .

The Kansas Beef Boom

Five miles of longhorns on the move, walking at a slow, steady pace from Texas to Kansas.

The earliest of the Long Drives left Texas in 1866. Ranchers learned that an eastern railroad line had reached as far west as Sedalia, Missouri. It was good news. From there, cattle could be loaded in stock cars and shipped cheaply to Chicago (a meat packing center) or New York. It was a busy spring. Every rancher in Texas was out on the range land searching for mavericks, branding all the cattle he could locate, lining up men for the trail drive. In that one season, some 260,000 head of cattle made their way northward along the Shawnee Trail — through Dallas, crossing Indian Territory (later to become the state of Oklahoma), and into southeastern Kansas.

That's where trouble began.

Texas longhorns were well known for carrying a tick that caused Texas fever in cattle. The longhorns weren't bothered, but for Kansas cattle the virus was deadly.

To protect local livestock, both Kansas and Missouri had enacted quarantine laws prohibiting longhorns from passing through during the summer months when ticks were active. But since it would be insanity to think any cattle could survive a Kansas winter, the Texas drovers took their chances. If it couldn't be summer, it would be never.

Kansas farmers answered their bravado with shotguns.

Worse than that, a lawless breed of "jayhawkers" used the law to waylay herds, beat up the cowhands and steal the cattle.

Jim Daugherty was herding his cattle to Kansas when a gang of jayhawkers waylaid him, killed one cowboy, tied him to a tree and whipped him until he agreed to return to Texas.

All this was a serious deterrent to any thought of future cattle drives.

19

Hopeless as it seemed, they were saved by one of those rare turns of luck that everyone prays for. Joseph G. McCoy (yes, the "real McCoy") came up with the answer. He created the largest cattle market in history. He did it using two pieces of information. First, rail lines had now extended well into Kansas. Second, Kansas had changed its quarantine law to permit Texas cattle anywhere west of the settled farm lands.

That's all McCoy needed.

A prodigious mover-and-shaker, he persuaded the Kansas Pacific Railroad to set special rates for shipping cattle from Kansas to Chicago. For the shipping point he picked Abilene, a small, dusty dot on the Kansas landscape.

He bought land for shipping yards, he bought lumber to build holding pens and loading chutes and a hotel. He sent scouts to Texas to spread the word about Abilene. Then, in what must be the greatest publicity stunt of the century, he loaded a 2,300-pound longhorn bull in a railroad car, accompanied by a Wild West show, and sent the lot to Chicago with a banner reading

ABILENE KANSAS
THE MARKET FOR TEXAS CATTLE

Wherever the train stopped along the route, people lined up to stare in wonder at the amazing **Texas longhorn.**

Cattle buyers flocked to Abilene. The route from Texas to Abilene, known as the Chisholm Trail, became the most famous cattle trail of the West. And Abilene became one of the first of the wild, end-of-trail towns of the wild, Wild West.

The trail drive wasn't over until the steers had been forced through a chute into rail cars, hustled along by a poke from the cowboy's stick. That gave him a new name – cowpoke.

Livery Stable Abilene

This was the Golden Age of the Cowboy West, you might say the very birthday of the cowboy as a distinct type in America. True, he had been operating in Texas for many years before that. But with increasing markets for stock now definitely established, the Long Trails were the proving grounds of the cowboy.

He was met by Middlewesterners with a certain amount of antagonism. His breezy, unconventional, swaggering personality, and the great hordes of longhorns that came with him, did not win him a warm welcome. But there was no stopping him. The Long Trails were being slowly and indelibly engraved on the virgin sod of the prairies. And the Chisholm Trail, named after a half-breed Cherokee who used it as a wagon trail, established itself as the epitome, legendary symbol of the Great Cattle Trail Era.

The cowboy's hard, sometimes dangerous, life produced a raw sense of humor that especially appreciated the ignorance of greenhorns.

Godfrey Sykes, an English immigrant who aspired to the romantic life of the cowboy, secured his first job when an old hand became ill and couldn't go up trail. Since he didn't have his own bedroll yet, he was given the blankets of the sick man. "When we reached Dodge City the herd owner came up and asked about my health and if I had felt any sickness on the trail. Then he told me — and both he and the trail foreman seemed to think it a rather good joke — that the sick man whose blankets I had been sleeping in, had been in a rather advanced stage of small pox when he dropped out. He said he had been relying on the air of the plains and the bean-pot of the cook to ward off infection."

"As long as there's a cow out there, and a horse to get on, and people to eat beef, there will always be cowboys."

After two or three months on the trail, wearing the same grimy jeans, mud-caked boots and sweat-stained hat, the boys were heartily sick of trying to out-think the stupid longhorn, fed up with dangerous, monotonous work, tired of confronting nature in its various forms on a diet of beans, bacon and biscuits, and getting edgy with the company of only each other and the cows.

Then, one day, looking beyond the sea of longhorns, a few wisps of chimney smoke were spotted, and the flickering lamps that spelled the trail's end. Abilene wasn't much of a town, but to the long-suffering cowhand, it looked like New York City.

Each man knew what he needed most when he hit town, and it wasn't either drink or women.

There were few razors in a trail outfit, and about the only chance for a bath was in fording the muddy streams. He looked like an animated doormat and smelled to high heaven. So first he wanted a haircut and a shave, followed by a bath and clean clothes. Next he wanted a good meal. Then, clean, full and well dressed, he set out in search of fun and adventure.

———

The merchants of Abilene tried to furnish everything he might want.

———

Because whiskey and cow work didn't mix, a strict rule of cattle country was "no whiskey with the wagon." Consequently, when the trail rider got to town he had developed a serious case of "bottle fever." With spurs jingling, boots clacking and loud-mouthed kidding, each one tried to squeeze through the swinging doors ahead of the other.

> *The cowboy didn't drink a lot; his line of work didn't permit it. But once he got the opportunity, he had a prodigious thirst.*
>
> *One story — probably exaggerated — told about two cowhands who had saved their money for a few years and went to a little cattle-shipping town and bought the only saloon. They closed the place for what the locals thought was a redecorating job. But after a week passed and the place still didn't open, the thirsty began to gather in front and holler at them to open the place. One of the cowboy owners got tired of the noise out front and went to the door. "When you goin' to open up?" asked one of them. "Open, hell," answered the new saloon owner. "We bought this joint to do our own drinkin'."*

Yet these long-awaited pleasures weren't available for everyone right away. Somebody had to watch over all those cows, and if the trail herd arrived behind a lot of other outfits, the cattle might have to be held a half-dozen miles from town. It was sheer agony for the men on watch to sit in the saddle, grimy as ever, staring at the lights of the distant pleasure palaces, dreaming of what they might be missing.

But sooner or later, every man had his chance. Often it was the only opportunity of the year to whoop it up, and he grabbed at it with a whooping, pistol-firing vengeance.

Recorded in the 1886 " Annals of Kansas" is a contemporary view: "Well-mounted and full of their favorite beverage, the cowboys dash through the principal streets, yelling like Comanches. This they call 'cleaning out a town.' "

The trail boss well knew that a rollicking, riotous trail-end town was paradise for gamblers, girls and gunmen, and in an effort to tame his men's exuberance he usually advanced only enough money to last until night time, in the hope that they'd be back in camp by then.

But some were lucky in gambling for a while, and as the night wore on and the liquor began to take hold, they were likely to resent the authority of the marshal, to get to fussing with each other, and turn into whooping hellions seeking to hurrah the town with gunfire, just for relaxation and entertainment.

Abilene Frolics

Few more wild, reckless scenes can be seen on the civilized earth than a dance house in full blast in one of the frontier cowtowns. Joseph McCoy, who brought the cowboy to Abilene and had a frequent close-up look at the scene, has given a good account:

To say they dance wildly or in an abandoned manner is putting it mild. Their manner of practicing the terpsichorean art would put the French can-can to shame.

The cowboy enters the dance with a peculiar zest, not stopping to divest himself of his sombrero, spurs, or pistols, but just as he dismounts off of his cow pony, so he goes into the dance. A more odd, not to say comical sight, is not often seen than the dancing cowboy; with the front of his sombrero lifted at an angle of fully forty-five degrees; his

huge spurs jingling at every step or motion; his revolvers flapping up and down like a retreating sheep's tail; his eyes lit up with excitement, liquor and lust; he plunges in and "hoes it down" at a terrible rate, in the most approved yet awkward country style; often swinging "his partner" clear off of the floor for an entire circle, then "balance all" with an occasional demoniacal yell, near akin to the war whoop of the savage Indian. All this he does, entirely oblivious to the whole world "and the balance of mankind." After dancing furiously, the entire "set" is called to "waltz to the bar," where the boy is required to treat his partner, and, of course, himself also, which he does not hesitate to do time and again, although it costs him fifty cents each time.

During the cattle season, from May to September, the main business of Abilene was the entertainment of drovers – and people flocked to supply it. In April 1871 the population was no more than 500; three months later it had swelled to 7,000.

Abilene's whiskey and gambling profits soared to unimagined heights. The coaches of the primitive railroad were arriving jammed with fast women, three-card monte throwers and liquor salesmen. Trade was particularly brisk at the Alamo, most spirited and ornate of Abilene's 20 sluicing spots, with a reported two dozen bartenders on duty around the clock, and three orchestras.

It didn't take long to get the cowboy's money out of circulation.

Gamblers knew the lure of the games for the cowboy, and they had the cards stacked and ready for him. For the cowboy, somehow there were never enough spots on the cards; luck kept sitting on the dealer's shirt tail. It seemed the best he could hold was some very young clubs, while the dealer could always seem to outhold a warehouse. If he did happen to draw a hand of two pair or three of a kind, the dealer would show him a hand of five, all wearing the same complexion. By evening's end, the cowboy could usually count his coin without taking it from his pocket.

All this uninhibited hurrah was distasteful to the rest of Kansas, and eventually a law was pushed through the state legislature forbidding the loading of cattle at Abilene. The cattle shippers then moved on to Hays City down the railroad line, and later to more westerly towns like Ellsworth and Newton, Wichita and Dodge City. They all flourished for a few years with a certain mystique of glamour. As boomtowns, they were unique in American history; they sprouted where Texas cattle trails intersected with the westward-moving railroads. At the outset, virtually everything about them was designed to handle longhorns and to assuage the frustrations of the Texas cowboy. Some lived but a year, others such as Dodge City grew into bona fide cities. But the entire phenomenon lasted no more than twenty years.

All the aspects of the trail cowboy in time became a legend — the gun toting, extravagant gambling, hurrahing of main streets, riding horseback into taverns, free spending and free-wheeling — and above all, the cowboy's loyalty to the outfit.

It all started with Abilene.

Code of the Cowboy

In the 1860s, the western half of the country was a big, empty land (six inhabitants per square mile) where formal law was sketchy at best. So early cowboys developed their own code of behavior, and took pride in upholding this unwritten code. Failure to abide didn't bring formal punishment, but the man who broke it became more or less a social outcast.

One of the first rules of the code was courage. A cowpuncher's life was full of dangers such as mad cows, swollen rivers, treacherous quicksands and unfriendly Indians. A coward endangered lives.

☆

A strict range law was "no whiskey with the wagon." Nothing got a man fired quicker than drinking while working cattle.

☆

Grumblers didn't flourish in a cow camp. That didn't fit in with the code. Privations and hardships were endured without complaint. No one knew if a man was tired. Sickness or injury were his own secret. In one camp, a cowboy returned to the bunkhouse, sat down and began to whittle a stick. After he had shaved it thin, he bared his leg and revealed a deep wound. His horse had stumbled, he said, and his gun had gone off accidentally. That brief explanation over, he wrapped a rag around the stick, pushed it into the wound to scrape out the gunpowder, then rode 30 miles to a doctor with his leg across the saddlehorn.

☆

Loyalty was paramount. Once a cowhand had signed up with an outfit, he was "faithful to the brand." He worked long hours and packed no timepiece. No man stood over him. He'd ride night herd as faithfully on a rainy night or in stinging sleet as he would on starry, moonlit nights.

In trail days, a standing rule was to wake a man by speech and not by touch; the hardships of the drive frayed nerves and he was apt to come alive with a gun in his hand.

☆

When two men met, spoke, and passed on, it was a violation of the code for either to look back over his shoulder. Such an act was interpreted as an expression of distrust.

☆

Though the life was rugged, the tribulations were part of the game, and the cow puncher could usually see the funny side. His wry wit is part of the cowboy legend. Most of his humor depended upon the poker face with which he attempted to affect seriousness, and it was especially sharp when another had failed in an undertaking. The clumsy one never got sympathy. In one instance, when a roper had missed his throw at a steer for the third time, another cowhand rode up and asked, "Say, why don't you put a stamp on it and send it to him by mail?" Often humor relieved a tense situation. It probably solved more problems than the six-gun ever did.

☆

The obligation of friendship was deeper than all others. Yet he stood ready to offer friendly service to strangers. The rule required that whoever caught a signal of distress was to render quick assistance.

Utterly Utilitarian

Everything the cowboy wore was designed for use, not ornament. His pants were of material that could stand rough use. He wore them tight so they'd stay up without support — suspenders interfered with his work, belts could cause hernia when riding a pitching horse. A coat hampered freedom of movement, but he always wore a vest — not for warmth, but for storage room, to pack matches, short pencil and a tally book to keep track of cattle and salary due, a plug of tobacco or sack of makings. That Bull Durham tag hanging outside his pocket was a sign of his calling.

He'd spend as much as four months' wages on his hat; it was his proudest possession and was seldom removed. A seasoned cowboy could tell what state a man was from by the size and shape of his hat.

His boots were the most expensive part of his rigging, custom-made of high-grade leather. Heels were high so he could "dig in" when roping on foot, narrow and sloped so he could get loose from the stirrup if thrown. The sole was thin so he had the feel of the stirrup (he never planned to walk anywhere anyway). The vamp had to be skin-tight so his feet would look small — a point of pride with the cowboy, who never wanted to be mistaken for a "sodbuster."

Chaps protected his legs from thorns, brush scrapes and rope burns. He preferred a type that could be snapped on without removing his spurs. Spurs, though highly practical, were also a vital part of the cowboy's image, and he rarely took them off.

In short, every piece of apparel was utterly utilitarian.

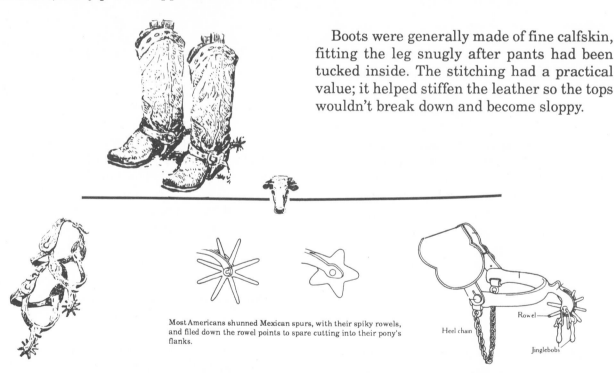

Boots were generally made of fine calfskin, fitting the leg snugly after pants had been tucked inside. The stitching had a practical value; it helped stiffen the leather so the tops wouldn't break down and become sloppy.

Most Americans shunned Mexican spurs, with their spiky rowels, and filed down the rowel points to spare cutting into their pony's flanks.

Rowel

Heel chain

Jinglebobs

Spurs were worn, not for punishment to the horse, but to get him moving in a hurry. Any man who mistreated his horse didn't last long in any outfit. There was a preference for large spurs (easier on the horse) with the points filed down.

But what the cowboy really liked about spurs was the nice jingle they made when he walked. Adding "jingle bobs" (danglers) made a sound that was music to any strutting cowboy's ears.

Hats

When John B. Stetson designed his famous ten-gallon hat, he gave the cowboy his most personal and prized possession. He was seldom without it. Its broad brim kept his shoulders dry in rain and shaded in sun. It was useful to fan a campfire or to carry water, and could distract a charging bull when thrown in its face. He called it his J.B., and he wanted the best he could afford.

Britches were made of heavyweight blue denim, and his favorite pants were Levis. They were "men's clothes." His shirt was made of gray cotton or flannel and had no collar.

Chaps were simply two wide trouser legs made of leather and connected by a narrow string that held them together in front. In northern climes, chaps made of fur or angora kept him warm, but could be miserable if they got wet or iced with snow. Real cowboys didn't wear chaps to town; they left them hanging in the bunkhouse.

Closed leg   Angora

The bandana was no mere ornament. It had more uses than anything the cowboy wore — a fine tourniquet, bandage, or sling. In a dust storm it could be a mask. Placed wet under his hat, it cooled his head. It was a towel when he washed his face in a water hole, or a mop when sweat ran from his brow. Spread over a muddy water hole, it was a strainer to drink through. A cowboy never went anywhere without his bandana.

The yellow slicker could be a rider's best friend. Any picture of a mounted cowboy wouldn't look quite natural without it tied behind the saddle. It kept the man from getting soaked when it rained; when he had to leave his saddled horse in the rain, he threw the slicker across the saddle to keep it dry. The horse didn't like it though. It didn't seem natural for the rider to make those crackling noises.

Round 'em Up!

Roundup was the most exciting time of a cowboy's job.

There were two roundups each year, in spring and fall, but the spring roundup was the big, important one. Over the winter, cattle of several brands grazed on the open range and got mixed together. The aim of the roundup was to sort them out by the brand they wore, and to brand the new calves.

Such roundups were large, complicated operations, sometimes involving as many as twenty ranches, each of which sent a crew of cowboys to the central camp. Two or three hundred cowboys would normally take part, plus two or three thousand horses.

For cowboys, this was the great social event of the year.

Here old cronies met after a year — or years — of not seeing each other. The air echoed with greetings — "If it ain't...!" — and old hands would throw their arms around the shoulders of cowpunchers that were new. Men with names like Curly Kid Davis or Bean Belly Bill shouted friendly insults at one another. There were roping contests, practical jokes, and stories around the campfire. One joke that never failed to get a laugh was to tie a man's spurs to a log, then wake him up by banging on a frying pan. By the light of the campfire, some man with a gift of gab might get up and tell about his adventures, true or not. A real story teller could spellbind his audience.

But on the night before roundup, the men knew they'd need all the sleep they could get. They knew that in the days ahead they'd never get enough sleep. They stretched out flat on the ground, a blanket beneath them, a tarp over.

Before daybreak, the cook hollered, "Damn your souls, get up!" The hands downed two or three cups of coffee strong enough to float an egg, the wrangler appeared with the remuda, and the roundup began. The great circle drag was on.

The cowboy lived on a monotonous and vitamin-deficient diet of beef, bacon, biscuits and beans – the latter wistfully known as "prairie strawberries."

The cowman never had more need of a cowboy than on the roundup. It required a special ability to bring in cattle from the roughest or most densely covered country. It demanded a quick eye and good judgment as well as mere ability to ride.

Roundup horses were swift, sturdy animals, ideal for chasing cattle. Where others hesitated, they plunged into thick brush to drive cattle into the open. The cowboys rode several miles in each direction, forming a circle with their camp at the center. Reaching their assigned positions, they fanned out and began to close in. Slowly the circle tightened, forcing the cattle toward the camp. Men working the outer circle were given an early start.

On the out trip each man tried to save his horse, to be in good shape for the hazing of cattle from the brush. If the terrain was rough, he might "smoke 'em out" of hiding places by firing a gun. Each man had to hunt out all the cattle on the ground to which he had been assigned.

As roundup advanced, the strain on the men grew greater, their hours longer. Few were on duty less than twelve to fifteen hours at a stretch.

As cattle gathered together, they were driven toward a holding spot. Back and forth through the dust the men swung and charged, swooping wide to round in a galloping steer, flinging their sweating horses at the congested herd. Uncertain calves, not knowing what to expect, lumbered awkwardly in a half-hearted gallop after their mothers. The mother broke into a long-drawn bawl to her calf.

All this bawling and bellering, the crackling of horns and pounding of hoofs, the dusty whirl of worried cattle, was part of the roundup.

Meanwhile, smoke rises from the branding area, and work will begin in earnest.

A collection of irons representing each stockman in the roundup lie by a blazing fire, over which one or two men work to keep the brands hot. Expert ropers ride up, each dragging a bawling calf, while its mother stands off at a safe distance and watches. A cowboy at the fire seizes the calf by its head, turns it over with an upward twist, secures its legs. Then the brand, not red-hot but still searing the quivering flesh of the calf, is pressed. A knife adds such additional marks as the owner has adopted, probably a notch cut in an ear, which makes it easier for a riding cowboy to recognize than a brand, in a milling herd of cattle.

No matter what the brand, putting it on hurt. As soon as the iron met flesh, the calf bellowed.

When the circle riders had driven the cattle into the holding spot, the concentrated mass was then invaded by cowboys on cutting horses. This called for bold and skillful riding. It was hard, wearing work, keeping man and horse constantly on the alert. Only three or four men did the cutting because too many riders could get the cattle stirred up so that mothers and calves got separated from each other.

Cutting 'em Out

The cutting horses were the most responsible and skillful horses on the range, alert and so intelligent that their riders had little need of reins, actually more concerned that over-guidance might break the horse's concentration. As soon as the man showed the pony what calf or steer he wanted to pull out of the herd, the horse's ears began to twitch, and its eyes would stay glued to the pursued animal while it was being chased toward the branding fire. Horse and rider worked as unobtrusively as possible, to keep the herd still and the calves with their mothers. "The horse perceives at once which is the calf to be ejected," said a Montana cowman. "If the calf turns, your horse wheels around, always keeping between it and the herd, till she gives it up and runs to the 'cut,' where you want her."

Cattle separated from the herd might be for shipping, or branding of mavericks, or to separate cows whose calves were unbranded.

In cowboy language, any cattle culled out for shipment would be called a "beef cut." Calves and mothers would be "a cut of cows with calves" and put in a separate area. The men in control were said to be "holding the cut" and this was a job for vigilance, as cut cows had a definite preference for getting back to the main herd.

The work would continue without letup. Each team worked under the midday sun; the smell of sweat, blood, and burned hair hovered in the air. A tally man, appointed by the roundup boss, kept record of the calves as they were branded. He had the opportunity to falsify records if he favored one particular ranch. But in the rude ethics of the range, this possibility was never considered.

As the herd grew smaller and the tally-book marks multiplied, yearlings without a brand were dragged up to the fire. These were the "mavericks," that had escaped the dragnet of the last year's roundup. They were distributed according to the law of the range in proportion to the size of ranchers' herds.

Although most of the males were castrated, the tally man had the privilege of selecting a percentage of the choice bulls to be kept intact for breeding purposes, usually something like eight baby bulls for 100 heifers.

Toward the end of each afternoon the wagon moved on to a night camp. While a few men circled the herds, the others ate their final meal of the day. A few unlucky riders prepared to guard the cattle in shifts through the night. The rest of the crew bedded down on hard ground, cushioned by no more than a quilt-blanket, hoping it didn't rain or that unwelcome insects didn't join him under his tarp.

Les Moore, a Texas driver gives a vivid description of early cowhunts when he was a boy of 14:

We didn't call them roundups in those early days. We called them cow-hunts, and I was the only boy on this one, looking out for cattle that belonged to my father before the war. We had no wagon (chuck wagon). Every man carried his grub in a wallet behind his saddle, and his bed under his saddle. A wallet is a sack with both ends sewed up with a mouth of the sack in the middle. I carried a lot of extra wallets, and a string of tin cups on a hobble around my pony's neck. Whenever the boss herder couldn't hear those cups jingling, he'd come around and wake me up. At night I carried brush and corn stalks and anything I could get to make a light for those who were on guard to play poker by. My compensation for light was twenty-five cents per night or as long as the game lasted.

TYPICAL BRANDS

Arizona cowman Evans Coleman claims he has known cowhands "who could not read or write, but who could name any brand on a cow." A brand was the key to ownership. The components of a brand were always read from left to right, from top to bottom. Coleman swore a good cowboy could understand "the Constitution of the United States if it were written with a branding iron on the side of a cow."

When the 1873 bank crash wiped out Charles Goodnight, he ran into good fortune – literally – when John Adair, an ebullient Irishman, put up $500 million to be his partner. The brand on the beef was JA.

Biggest ranch of all was the XIT, which occupied three million acres, hired 150 cowboys who rode 1,000 horses to herd 150,000 head of cattle. Their XIT branded 35,000 calves a year.

When a gunslinger arrived in the West he had nothing to his name but a two .45-caliber pistols. Later he made good as a cattleman, and memorialized 45 into his brand.

Selecting a brand was no small endeavor. Sometimes the ranch itself was named after the brand. In this case, the rancher formed a brand that spelled his name – Barwise.

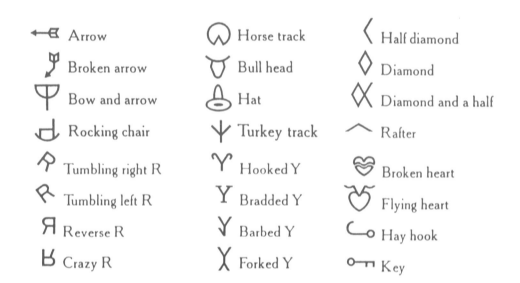

Arrow

Broken arrow

Bow and arrow

Rocking chair

Tumbling right R

Tumbling left R

Reverse R

Crazy R

Horse track

Bull head

Hat

Turkey track

Hooked Y

Bradded Y

Barbed Y

Forked Y

Half diamond

Diamond

Diamond and a half

Rafter

Broken heart

Flying heart

Hay hook

Key

Tall Grass in the North

When quarantine laws finally outlawed
Texas cattle from the entire state of Kansas, a
new trail had to be established to rail lines.

The Goodnight-Loving trail bypassed Kansas, cut through New Mexico Territory, Colorado, Wyoming Territory, and into Montana Territory as far as Miles City. No one ever believed, though, that these vast, lonesome plains had any value for ranging cattle. The blizzard-driven winters were too punishing for animals.

Then a strange winter accident in Colorado, unrelated to trail drives, changed the course of cattle-industry thinking.

An ox-drawn wagon train freighting goods from Kansas to the Rockies was halted by heavy snows. Unable to go forward, the drivers cached the wagons, turned the oxen loose, and gave up. Next spring they returned with new oxen to replace those left to die. They found the oxen contentedly chewing grass, sleek and alive. Here was proof, indeed, that cattle could thrive in cold northern plains. When cross-country rail lines were established two years later, cattlemen were the first to invade the golden land. Great herds, the foundations of great fortunes, were quickly established.

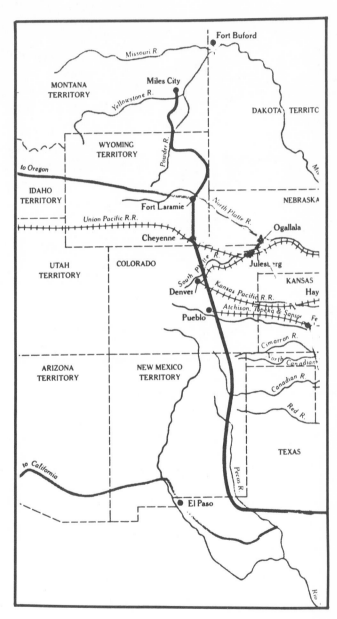

The Good-night Loving Trail from Texas to Miles City, Montana

On the northern ranches, the method of operating was quite different from that on the Texas spreads. The long drives to distant railroads were no longer a concern. The main job was to fatten cattle for market and to nurse them through the bitter winters.

Now the cowboy's life changed too. Cattle barons operating tens of thousands of cattle on hundreds of thousands of acres no longer looked for casual or temporary hands, but canny and farsighted permanent employees — men who carefully separated and sorted out breeding cattle, who gentled a herd for maximum growth, who cut and stored hay for use as winter feed.

Early Texas roundups were informal, mainly concerned with locating scattered stock in rough brush. It was different in the North, where enormous herds crossed divides and mingled with other herds. Glancing around, a man on any given range might see nary a cow. In 1885, a tongue-in-cheek story in a Colorado paper announced that Colorado ranchers hoped to solve roundup problems by importing a telescope powerful enough to read brands on cattle 150 miles away.

A Colorado cowpuncher cradles a weakened, motherless calf he found stranded.

35

A cowboy's life didn't soften much, though.

His home was the bunkhouse, often just a shack of cottonwood logs — cold in winter, hot and smelly in summer. The interior was generally covered with newspapers. It didn't keep out the winter cold, but reading the walls helped the puncher kill boredom.

There's an air of hominess about this bunkhouse papered with newsprint — demure pinups, cattle charts, photos from home, keepsakes, a thermometer, a photo draped in black.

Out on the range the cowboy fried his brains under the summer sun, keeping his cattle on good grass, shoeing horses, putting out salt, repairing windmills, riding endless miles in rain and wind looking for lost calves. He was a part-time vet who invented his own cures using powerful medicine like carbolic acid.

One of the most onerous chores was bog riding in spring, when the pesty heelfly drove cattle to run for the nearest bog hole to escape the torturous bites. Once bogged, they couldn't free themselves. The suction of the soil held the animal's feet as if in a vise, and the more it struggled the deeper it sank. It took two cowhands to pull the cow out, one to rope and pull, the other to wade into the gumbo with a shovel to dig the cow's legs free, all the time keeping his own legs moving to keep from getting bogged himself.

Still, the land held them like a spell. William Timmons, who worked on the Goodnight ranch in Texas, heard tales around the Texas campfires about the northern range, told by cowboys who had ridden there and who had seen the northern lights, the tall free grass, swollen streams. He decided to cast his lot with the cowmen of the northern plains.

He never went back to Texas.

Cattle Barons

Although the cowboy was destined to become an American legend and the symbol of the epic Old West, he was not in the saddle for that reason. He was there because hard-headed businessmen decided they wanted to make money — lots of money — in cattle.

These men were the cattle barons. Some were Easterners, some came from England. Charlie Goodnight was different. He started out as a cowboy, and made it up the ladder as one of the greatest. He never forgot his beginnings; he knew what the cowboy's life was like.

In the words of William Timmons, one of his cowhands and a lifetime friend, "Charles Goodnight's name was the best known of any in the cattleman's West, his personality the most striking. Even rival cattlemen were proud of him, and settlers figured he outranked the President of the United States.

"I was fourteen year old when I saw Goodnight for the first time. The memory remains one of the most vivid of my life. I was working for his nephew, Walter Dyer, working with the horses. Walter was rough and gruff, especially when he had been drinking. One day I was cleaning out the horse barn, loading manure into a wagon to be dumped, but the mules pulling the wagon ran it into a gate post, wedging the post between the wheels so tight I couldn't back up and couldn't go forward.

"All I could do was unload it and start over. But even empty, I couldn't budge it. I was wondering what trouble I was going to be in with Walter, when a man drove up in a buckboard. I had never seen Mr. Goodnight before, but there was no mistaking who he was.

"He was a big man with great physical strength. Although he was in his middle fifties, his dark hair and beard were hardly touched with gray. Looking at his massive head, those burning eyes of his, his huge shoulders, his bowlegs, and his shuffling gait, I thought of old Sykes, the king of the buffalo herd that grazed behind a high wire fence on the Goodnight ranch.

"Mr. Goodnight easily lifted my wagon away from the gate post and helped me reload. We drove out to the field and he helped me unload. As we were driving back to the corral where his buckboard was, he asked if Walter was good to me. "No, sir," I replied. "But his helper Jim is."

"Well," he said, "tell Jim to send you over to my ranch tomorrow. You can work for me."

Goodnight lost a fortune when Indian raids wiped out his cattle fortune in Texas, then he made another one. Looking north, he saw greater opportunity. He blazed the Goodnight trail, one of the earliest to carry wiry Texas longhorns to northern markets and feeding grounds. After that came Goodnight's ranching activities in Colorado. By the time he was thirty-two, his fame was no longer confined to Texas. He had given his name to the West.

Not all cattle barons made it big. Several failed, but none so spectacularly as the Marquis de Mores, a fine figure of a man with black curly hair and mustaches waxed to pinpoints. Of royal blood, it was believed he wanted to make a fortune so he could overthrow the French government and become king. Out on the Dakota prairies, he lived in a 28-room mansion staffed with butlers on down to chambermaids. He had a great idea: save on freight costs by shipping the meat instead of the whole animal. He was ahead of his time, and lost millions of dollars of his father-in-law's money before returning to France.

One of the Marquis de Mores' neighbors was equally famous — Theodore Roosevelt, who aspired to being a cowboy. Seriously grieved by his wife's death, he went west in 1883 and bought a ranch in Dakota.

Cowboys scarcely knew what to make of him. Wearing thick glasses, and blessed with very large teeth, he became known as Four Eyes, or sometimes Toothadore. He had a tendency to call out "Bully!" when something particularly pleased him, or in his thick Harvard accent, "By Godfrey, this is fun!" On his first roundup he dashed about on his horse crying out, "Hasten forward quickly there!" That became the joke of the century to his cowboy friends, and for weeks afterward, they'd order one another to "hasten forward quickly there!"

But he earned the respect of his fellow cowboys because he was brave in danger and had endurance in tough situations. They also appreciated him when he was being taunted by a bully in the hotel saloon. Finally out of patience, Roosevelt muttered, "Well, if I've got to I've got to," rose from his chair and flattened the bully with a punch to the jaw.

To his dying day, Roosevelt thought of himself as a cowboy.

As a cattle baron, the Marquis de More had high aspirations. To promote his plan of shipping butchered meat, he built icehouses at four points along the railroad, then extensively promoted "Medora-killed beef" in Eastern cities. All that remains of his dream is the brooding chateau on a bluff overlooking the Little Missouri.

One of his first acts in his new North Dakota life was to have a local seamstress make him a buckskin shirt, which he said was "the most distinctively national dress in America." Later he added a broad sombrero, horsehide chaps, cowboy boots, and silver spurs.

Bronco Busting

The workhorse of the cowboy was the mustang, a small, wiry animal that roamed the open range free, in plentiful numbers. Although it didn't aspire to wear a saddle, that was to be its destiny.

Half wild and totally ornery, it was captured when about four years old, and put through a traumatic course of training that would break its will until it would obey its rider's every command.

The process was called bronc busting, and the cowboy who undertook the job faced a brutal struggle. Bronc busters were mostly young men. By the time they were thirty they were likely either dead or crippled or no longer cared to take the punishment. The saying was, "The buster maybe ain't strong on brains, but he ain't short on guts."

In early range days, when horses were plentiful and cheap, most busters would "rough break" them — rope, choke down, blindfold, and saddle a green bronc, then mount, strip off the blindfold, dig in with the spurs, slam the horse with a quirt, and proceed to fight it out until the animal was convinced it was better to behave than suffer the pain. Often this grueling, sweaty, dusty work was done by an itinerant who went from one ranch to the next offering his services. He was paid five dollars a horse. For that he could scarcely take the time to be gentle on the beast.

But later, the large outfits would keep a man or two on the payroll, paying him a bit more than the average cowhand, whose job was to break horses. He could take the time to go at it on a more gentle pace.

He might spend time teaching the bronc the terrors of the rope. He'd wrap the rope around the snubbing post in the center of the corral until the horse wearied of dashing to the end of the rope, and learned it was useless to fight the string.

Before putting a saddle on, he might "sack out" the horse — put a grain sack on its back and let him flip it until convinced the sack wouldn't hurt him. When the cowboy did put a saddle on him, he blindfolded it first. Then, as he mounted, he'd pinch the horse's ear to distract it by discomfort.

Even at that, it was no joyride to ride a bucking bronc.

SADDLING THE WILD HORSE

L.A. Huffman, a Montana photographer, captured this remarkable series of photos of Lee Warren, a contract bronc buster, at work. Six horses are channeled into the corral. They race about wildly looking for an exit, until Warren, swinging a wide loop, lays a noose around the neck of a beautiful bay, which he promptly dubs "Oscar Wilde" – a name that will stick with the horse to the end of his days.

The Flying Noose Falls True
Leaping, bucking, striking savagely at the thing that grips him by the throat, Oscar will soon be snubbed to a post. Straining against the rope, he throws himself. Warren tilts Oscar's head upwards, slips the noose over his ears bridle-wise, then deftly hobbles the front feet together and slips on the bridle. Soon the hind feet too are caught in the noose.

Cross-hobbled and Saddled
Now the bronc rider must lay a saddle blanket on the horse, and while holding reins and rope, swing a forty-pound saddle with one hand to the top of the horse. Dazed and cross-hobbled, the horse resents the blanket to the twentieth time, but eventually the saddle is firmly in place.

First Pull at the Latigo
Bridled and hobbled, the horse bucks at the first attempt to tighten the cinch. After a few hard pulls, the saddle is firmly in place, but Oscar continues to toil away for fifteen minutes – no doubt it seems longer – then his hobbles are removed. Often that task is as exciting as putting them on.

The Rider Hits the Saddle
The hobbles are off, but Oscar doesn't know it because Warren is distracting him by twisting his ear – a trick that will turn the wildest outlaw motionless for a minute or more. Warren swings lightly into the saddle. For several seconds, Oscar stands frozen, wide-eyed, then up he goes in a long, curving leap. Down goes his head, and he blats out that indescribable bawl that only terrified broncs can fetch, an uncanny sound that rasps the nerves.

Taming the Wild One
The horse sulks, then rears high to throw his mount. He cannot be allowed to succeed, for if the lesson is a failure, he will become Oscar the Outlaw. Warren has another tamer, one that he is loath to use – the rawhide quirt. Oscar gives up on punishment, deciding that walking the circle is a better choice. That ends the first lesson, but the next day Oscar will learn the lesson of the slicker. He must learn to ignore unexpected sounds and motions. Warren hazes the horse with a slicker, then rides him to a standstill.

Looking for a place to land

One of the first things a bronc rider learned was how to fall when thrown — "how to get off without getting a hoof stuck in his vest pocket," as an old cowhand said. He learned to kick free of the stirrups, to go limp and hit the ground rolling. He knew he was going to jump before he actually went, and tried to find a good spot to land — preferably not near cactus.

Whatever the bronc rider had to go through, one thing was certain, he was made of whalebone and rawhide. He didn't ride the rough ones just for a close-up view of the stars, but many a time some gut-twister had him soaring so high it was downright scary to a man without wings.

Riding a bucking horse was a contest requiring skill, courage and strength. But almost every ranch had one or more outlaw horses, broncos "as bad as ever wore hair" — attesting to the fact that a bronc buster wasn't successful every time.

No two horses bucked exactly alike. The majority bucked from fear, but some bucked because they felt the spur, or for the pure fun of it. Some bucked from pure viciousness. Those usually became outlaws and could never be tamed.

"Straightaway" buckers were big and strong; they jumped extremely high, then as they came down, kicked high with their hindquarters. They could hurt the rider seriously when bucking him off because they generally threw high and hard.

A horse that bucked in circles and figure-eights was called a "pioneer bucker" because it was always seeking new territory.

When a horse reared wildly and vaulted upward, pawing with its front feet, it was known as a "cloud hunter."

A "pile driver" was a horse that humped its back and came down with all four legs as stiff as ramrods. The result was a grinding shock that could drive a man's spine through his hat.

A "spinner" was a horse that bucked in tight circles, spinning in a small space, whirling and bucking with a backward motion that might cause the rider to become dizzy and lose his sense of balance. (He usually ended up "eating gravel.")

41

Come 'n Get it!

Like some oversized steer the old chuck wagon trailed along with the cowboys, an imperishable part of any Western ranching scene. On trail or roundup it served as a rolling commissary, crammed full of everything from bedrolls to spare bullets, beans to prunes. Standing fiercely by was the crabbed individualist who would sooner poison a finicky hand than look at him.

Wearing a flour-sack apron, he tended the coffee mill, fed his fire with buffalo chips or gathered branches, tended the Dutch oven with its sourdough biscuits rising. At mealtimes, on the ground next to the wagon, gathered the rough, sweaty crew that for more than one cowboy represented family.

Next to the trail boss, the cook was the highest paid member. He was usually an older cowboy who had given up his horse for the chuck wagon. They called him, usually, the Old Lady. Besides serving up three meals a day, he doctored wounds, shaved beards, cut hair, pulled teeth, and dispensed medicinal liquor as required. No one kept longer hours than the Old Lady. First to rise, he was the last to bed. On trail, his final duty was to turn the wagon to face the North Star, so that the trail boss would know which direction to head in the morning.

His food could make or break a trail drive. Good grub kept the men happy, poor food made them grumpy and derelict in their duties. That gave the cook tremendous power, and trail hands were careful to stay in his favor.

The chuck wagon itself was a monument to creativity. It was invented by Charles Goodnight, owner of the first ranch in the Texas Panhandle, who rebuilt if from a surplus Army wagon, which has extra durable iron axles. On the wagon bed, bulk foodstuffs were stored; on one side there was a water barrel big enough to hold two days' supply of water; on the other was a heavy tool box. Like a covered wagon, it had a canvas cover to protect it from sun and rain.

But the innovation that made the wagon unique was the installation of a chuck box at the rear of the wagon. It had a hinged lid that let down to form a work table for the cook. Above it was a box honeycombed with small storage cubbyholes. Here the cook could store the foods he needed for the day, and his pots and pans. A drawer above carried everything from calomel to sewing needles.

The design of the chuck wagon was so popular that everyone copied it, and eventually it was produced commercially by the famous Studebaker Company for $75.

On trail, most of the cook's repertoire had a dreary sameness — beans, bacon and biscuits. But on occasion, given beef to work with, he cooked savory gourmet dish known as sonofabitch stew, for which there were nearly as many recipes as there were range cooks. Mostly its ingredients were whatever was available to the cook at the moment, but was likely to contain cut-up heart, testicles, tongue, liver and marrow gut, which is the semi-digested contents of the tube connecting the ruminant's stomachs. Sweetbreads and brains might be added. To give it character, a healthy dose of Louisiana hot sauce was tossed in.

Woe to the ranch whose cook served up bad food, for top hands would not stay at such a place.

Swinging a Wide Loop

Jo Mora

Every cowboy had to have some roping ability to hold his job, and occasionally an unerring, quick throw saved a fellow puncher from injury by a mad cow. But tossing a lariat could be an art, and few mastered it.

A good roper had to have a sense of perfect timing, and the ability to judge distance. Calculating the speed of a running steer with that of his horse, he had to judge the amount of rope to span the distance between. Top ropers seemed to know by intuition the proper time to throw. They had an uncanny sense of knowing just when the loop would reach the animal's feet at the split second they'd be off the ground.

It took constant practice to coordinate this judgment. Watching a smooth roper at work was a beautiful sight. During branding, it was his job to heel the calves from horseback and drag them to the iron men. He went about his job methodically and coolly, and seldom missed.

He usually rode a steady horse, preferably one with a running walk or slow foxtrot. He eased through the herd, flipping his loop over the calf's head or heels with apparently little attention to where his rope was going. When he threw, his horse automatically turned toward the bulldoggers waiting to get the calf to the branding irons.

A lariat wasn't just some long piece of rope. It was the cowboy's most important tool, carefully handcrafted from either braided rawhide (expensive) or twisted tough grass. He used it to catch cattle, to hold his horse, to pull cows from bogs, to kill snakes.

A lariat had to be stiff enough so that when a broad loop was played out it could be sent flying toward its target still flat and open. And it had to be strong enough to take the wrenching shock of yanking a running thousand-pound steer.

The end of the rope was fashioned into a knot called the Honda, through which the loop could slide easily. For this purpose, grass was more practical than rawhide because it could make a knot, whereas a rawhide honda had to be specially crafted.

No matter how good a roper, much of his success depended upon a well trained rope horse. But roping on horseback was more dangerous than on foot. On foot the roper could always turn loose; but when a roped steer and a horse got tangled in a mixup, there wasn't much chance to leave the party.

Many of the throws of a good roper appear to be stunt tricks, but they served a useful purpose. The "figure eight" was a loop thrown so it would catch the forelegs of an animal in the lower part of the eight while the head was caught in the upper part.

The sketches **ahead** show how complicated the art of roping can be. But in actual practice, a cowhand who threw a steer too hard was likely to get called down by the boss. A heavy steer that turned a somersault at the end of a rope was likely to hit the ground with terrific force. Horns and even necks might be broken, or if the ground was hard, the steer could be bruised **so** badly it was worthless as meat.

The reata that Mexicans taught Texans to use was generally sixty feet long, but could be much longer. One vaquero even lassoed an eagle. A fancy roper could do remarkable things, like this tricky throw.

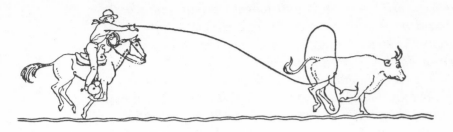

A powerful side-arm throw
with a big standing loop
circles the steer from behind.

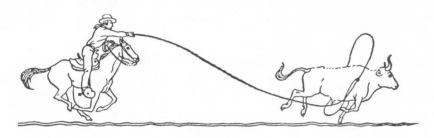

Loop travels forward
faster than the steer.

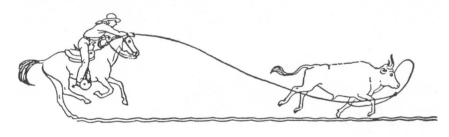

The lower part of the loop hits
the back of the steer's front legs,
clearing the steer's head.

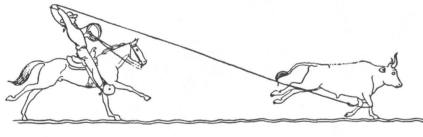

The roper quickly closes the loop.
Wraps the rope
around his saddle horn.

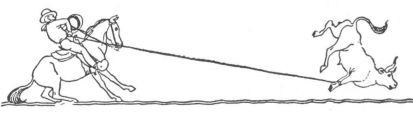

The pony squats
and the steer somersaults

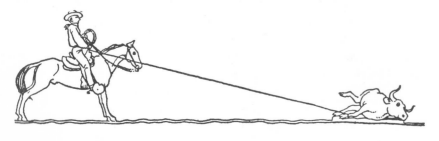

The steer is down before
he knows what hit him.

Fencing 'em In

In the 1880s, cattle-raising was being touted as the get-rich scheme of the decade, and everyone with a bankroll was eager to get in on the profits. Soon millions of cattle covered the ranges from Texas to Montana. The Texas Land & Cattle Company, for example, owned an area bigger than Long Island. Cattle were even put to graze on government lands. And to protect their holdings, owners started throwing barbed wire around all the land they claimed. If there was no river or stream on the property, they turned to windmills.

The open-range concept couldn't last forever. It came to an end when barbed wire was invented.

Now the cowboy had a new kind of chore — mending fences and keeping windmills pumping water. They called it "ridin' fence" and "ridin' mill." Along with it came "ridin' line." Spreads were now so big that they could no longer be operated from a central station. Someone had to be out in the far reaches, looking after things. It was the lonesome cowboy.

Lonesome, indeed.

The line rider's home, two or three months at a time, was a small shack, furnished with an iron-rail bed, a pine table covered with oilcloth, a few-straight-backed chairs and a small wood-burning stove in the kitchen. A slab of sowbelly hung from one wall, encrusted with salt. His eating tools were stashed within easy reach in a wooden box, along with an empty beer bottle for rolling out his biscuit dough.

Sometimes two men shared the line duty and the line cabin. They saw little of one another by day, but had company at night.

It's not a luxurious life. The line camp is about the size of a commodious jail cell, and furnished not much better.

Among the line rider's duties would be driving cattle away from patches of loco weed or alkaline water holes. If wolves were bad he set traps; if he saw a bitch wolf slinking, he might follow her to a den where her pups were hidden and dig them out. If he ran across an animal mired in a boghole, he had to rope it and pull it to dry ground. If he saw an overgrown calf nursing a mother too thin for her own good, he weaned the calf away so the mother could survive the winter.

In winter he had to chop holes in frozen water, working with cold hands and cold feet. At night he'd thaw himself out by cooking a hot meal then hit the blankets, never stopping to wonder why he was working so hard for $30 a month.

RIDIN' FENCE

"A whole lot of sorry things can happen to a fence," groused the old timer.

Sometimes lightning destroyed panels of fence. Bulls fighting on opposite sides of the fence could snap tightly-strung wires or push staples out and let wires sag. Erosion could deepen a hole large enough for cattle to crawl under. Gates might be left open.

The line rider carried tools the open-range cowboy would have balked at packing — pliers, cutters, hammer, a coil of wire. He got up early in the morning so he could do his chores and get on patrol by good daylight, and still get back to camp in time to grain his horses before dark.

Fence riding was a job for a man who could stand loneliness and his own cooking. Still, there were men who actually enjoyed being alone. "I loved to ride to a steep ledge, view the canyon at sunrise. I have fed wild turkeys and quail. The hoot of the owl and the howl of the coyote were music to my ears. My comrade was my horse."

The job, in short, attracts the kind of man who prefers hard work outdoors to comfort in a house, who enjoys solitude, who takes pride in exhaustion at the end of the day.

He is always busy because there is always fence to be ridden, and fence to be repaired, and wandering heifers to be caught.

But he lives in a wonder world where the hills cast long shadows in the evening and the stars in the sky are not out-dazzled by city lights.

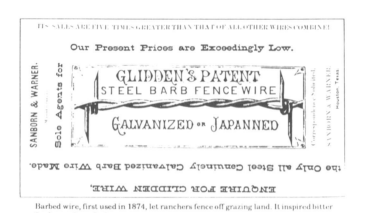

Barbed wire, first used in 1874, let ranchers fence off grazing land. It inspired bitter feuds over boundaries.

An old cowboy song declared barbed wire as Hell's own invention:

They say that Heaven is a free-range land
Good-by, good-by, O fare you well.
But it's barbed wire fence for the Devil's hat band
And barbed wire blankets down in Hell!

RIDIN' MILL

Nothing changed range life like the coming of the wire fence.

Fenced off from living water, something had to be done to bring water to the cattle. Water locators with their water witches began to come in, followed by the well drillers. Soon windmills started to dot the landscape.

The first windmills had a big wooden wheel, crude affairs without grease cups or oil reservoirs. They had to be greased by hand, and greased often. The rider knew what it needed before he got to it; the screeching of the wheel let him know a mile away.

Scrambling up the ladder with a beer bottle filled with oil, he'd drench the sucker rods and gears. Frequently he'd find the wheel whirling wildly with no water forthcoming, and he knew the sucker rod had broken. That meant hitching a horse to a block and tackle, haul out the rod, repair the break and start the mill again — all the while surrounded by milling cattle bawling out their thirst.

While he worked, the thirsty cattle tromped the troughs, hooked each other and made a general nuisance of themselves. He was grateful when he saw the water coming again – but then he had to fight the cattle to see what each had an opportunity to get its share.

With some simple alterations, any letter brand could become personalized.

Most windmills were 32 feet high, but some might be forty. It was dangerous work. Bowled off the top of the mill by a swinging vane, he could be killed or seriously injured. Most injuries, though, were caused by falling through rotten timbers.

Either way, he couldn't look forward to much in the way of medical help. Doctors were scarce, and medical treatment was often amateurish improvisation. Mostly a cowboy doctored himself. Sprained ankles could be cured by wrapping it in brown paper and soaking it with vinegar. Horse liniment sometimes did duty for the man who rode the horse. Deep cuts could be mended by a poultice of chewing tobacco. Most men survived.

The Cowboy as Hero

As the day of the open-range cowboy and those long trail drives started drifting into history, a strange phenomenon occurred. This lowly, hard-working herder of cattle began to turn into a romantic legend.

People in crowded cities, trapped on the treadmill of boring jobs, longed for the adventure, the excitement, the freedom they imagined in the cowboy's outdoor life, Easterners could never get enough of western lore. And to fire up their fantasies of the colorful, Wild West, a slew of magazines and cheap novels burst upon the scene.

The first of these writers was Ned Buntline, who turned Buffalo Bill Cody — sometime cowboy, scout and buffalo hunter — into a dime-novel hero. In a meeting with Buntline, Cody reeled off the many flamboyant details of his life, and Buntline went back to New York to embroider the already spectacular, overblown narrative.

These pulp-fiction cowboy stories achieved astounding popularity. Young boys were even running away from home to become cowboys. The firm of Beadle and Adams turned out some 2,200 titles — stories like Arizona Joe, Fred Fearnot in Colorado, Fancy Frank from Denver, Lariat Lil.

The Old West became big business in the twentieth century.

The action-filled life of the cowboy received enormous attention from novelists who wrote formula Westerns that didn't focus on the everyday life of the cowboy, but emphasized action and gunplay.

Zane Grey, a New York dentist, visited Arizona early in the century on a buffalo-hunting expedition and thus started a career writing books like "Riders of the Purple Sage," set in the coarse canyon and mesa country. It was one of the most popular Westerns ever written.

His first encounter with Arizona was brief, but its impact was permanent. The majestic mountains and the mysterious canyon near Flagstaff introduced him to a world completely different from anything he had encountered in the East. From then on, Arizona became the setting for his novels, and the name Zane Grey became almost synonymous with the West. Using plots, themes and characters he found in Arizona, he created an image that fascinated readers. He saw the shadow of the Old West, not its substance. An idealized West was the legend Zane Grey created, and his name became part of the legend.

But nothing enflamed "cowboy fever" like Buffalo Bill's Wild West Show, an extravaganza created by Bill Cody in 1883, that traveled from coast to coast and to several European cities. For a dime, spectators could see roping exhibitions, trick riding, mock cowboy/Indian battles, even Annie Oakley, who shot cigarettes out of men's mouths and coins from between their fingers.

Cody's troupers included real Indian braves, real cowboys, even a real marshal — Wild Bill Hickok — as well as his own fancy riding and roping.

The show also served as an impetus to popularize rodeo, a contest that had begun during days of the roundup, when cowboys from various ranches staged events to prove which cowboy could ride the roughest broncs, who was the best roper. In time, rodeos were held yearly in various western towns. The first regular rodeo began in 1888 in Prescott, Arizona.

One of the all-time greats was Bill Pickett, a black cowboy, who invented bulldogging. Picket would chase a longhorn, leap onto its back, and pull it down. He then would bite the struggling animal on its lower lip and jerk it flat on the ground.

Cody even recruited Chief Sitting Bull, paid him $50 a month plus all the money he could make independently having his picture taken. The Chief especially enjoyed the spectacle of the performing horses — in particular a gray dancing horse, which became a gift from Cody when the Chief completed his tour with the show. Four years later, in a skirmish with army cavalry at home on the reservation, shots were fired, the horse that Sitting Bull was riding mistook them for his cue and started dancing, and the Chief was killed in the melee.

Bill Pickett's most sensational performance was at Madison Square Garden in 1905, taming a boomer of a steer. As soon as the chute opened, the steer jumped the arena fence, crashed into the grandstand and kept bolting upward, pursued by the shouting Pickett on a willing horse. Right behind him was his mounted attendant — the hazer — an Oklahoma cowboy. The hazer roped the steer's heels, Pickett grabbed the head, and the two maneuvered and dragged the steer down into the arena. News photographers shot the scene, and the young hazer was identified as a trick roper of the Wild West show circuit — Will Rogers.

The Cowboy Philosopher

"Every man has wanted to be a cowboy"
...Will Rogers

No cowboy, before or since, has achieved the lasting fame of Will Rogers.

In his lifetime he straddled the timeline between driving cattle down dusty trails as a hard-working cowboy, and a world-famous show business legend whose career sprouted from his expertise as a roper and rider.

Growing up on his father's ranch in Oklahoma Territory on land governed by the Cherokee Nation, Will was taught by a freed slave on the ranch how to use a lasso as a tool to work Texas Longhorns. But Will fell in love with the lariat, and soon nothing on the ranch was beyond the reach of his rope. He'd rope anything, man, beast or fowl -- goats, geese, dogs, running sheep, and the hats of passing cowhands. Some of the tricks he perfected have never been duplicated. He could throw a rope around the waist of a passing rider -- not by throwing the rope over the rider's head, but under the feet of the galloping horse, then drawing it up to the rider,

Will Rogers was probably the most beloved man of his time, and certainly the world's best known private citizen. His boyish charm, his homespun but incisive wit and wisdom, his humility, his love for life and his genuine fascination with people, all made him irresistible.

"I'm just an ol' country boy trying to get along," he claimed. "I've been eating pretty regular, and the reason I have been is because I stayed an ol' country boy."

Actually, Will Rogers was much more than that. He was probably the greatest trick roper the world has ever seen, a vaudeville performer, an author, newspaper columnist, radio commentator, aviation promoter, movie star. But no role suited him better than that of philosopher and humorist.

He got his first audience laughter while performing rope tricks on a stage as a young man. Something went wrong, and young Will drawled, "Now, folks, this is a pretty good stunt if I can do it." The audience roared. They thought the mishap was part of the act. And with that, Will Rogers discovered his true gift: He could make people laugh. His often-stumbling cowboy commentary warmed crowds. He lambasted politics with a sort of aw-shucks modesty that enhanced a sophisticated wit. "Once a man holds public office he is absolutely no good for honest work," he wrote.

His knack for spinning off the news of the day to say what was on people's minds made him the most popular man in America in the 1920s. He was Hollywood's biggest draw for years and a columnist with 35 million readers who waited, daily, to see what "that card" Will Rogers had to say. He gave generously to down-at-the-heel cowboys and liked to relax by roping cows on his California ranch.

"Live your life so that when you die," he said, "they can give the family parrot to the biggest gossip in town."

Courtesy of Will Rogers Memorial and Birthplace

The Will Rogers Memorial Museum in Claremont, Oklahoma celebrates the life of Oklahoma's most famous native son -- his cowboy days in Oklahoma and Texas, and his stint as a gaucho in Argentina, before he joined the Wild West show that launched him as a famous performer, as well as his later life as a world personality. His birthplace is located 10 miles north in Oologah and is open for tours.

But it was movies that spread "the spirit of the West" worldwide.

They also provided a new source of income for cowboys. In Hollywood they could earn $7.50 a day — considerably better than ranch work — in all sorts of films using riders. A few even became stars.

William S. Hart was the first of them, the first genuine westerner to win stardom in a cowboy costume. He had spent his boyhood in Sioux lands, had seen frontier life at first hand, worked as a ranch hand, and had a deep appreciation for life in the wilds. He insisted on authenticity, and scored a great triumph as The Virginian. Hart's cowboys wore dusty clothes, lived in grim saloons, in towns that were drab and ramshackle.

But Hart's realism began to pall with moviegoers. In the 1930s they had problems of their own; they were looking for action and escape, and they wanted the good guys to triumph. Directors realized that a cowboy in the midst of his herd had no mystique and made for dull copy. So they gave the lads blazing six-shooters and plenty of opportunity to use them.

William S. Hart

Next to ride high were the pure action features and serials of such range hands as Tom Mix and Hoot Gibson, Ken Maynard and Buck Jones, who had spent some time around Hollywood and Wild West shows as stunt riders. Mix had been a Texas Ranger, Gibson punched cattle in Colorado, and Tim McCoy, another genuine western article, owned a Wyoming ranch.

Buck Jones

Hoot Gibson

Each portrayed the cowboy in a different light, giving their interpretation of the legend.

Tom Mix, most famous of the lot, was especially adept at turning out lean films with fast-breaking plots and almost nonstop action. He turned the cowboy into a sort of Robin Hood who, chasing bad guys all over the landscape and rescuing frontier maidens, just didn't have time for the gritty work of the West — mending fences and rounding up strays. He did most of his own stunt work, and had a reputation for taking risks that resulted in injury.

Off-screen, Tom Mix lived in flamboyant style far removed from his straight-shooting screen self, in a mansion, hobnobbing with European nobility.

Hoot Gibson, playing a different cowboy role, came up with an offbeat hero, the westerner who rarely carried a gun and was as apt to settle his problems by comic means as by action.

Buck Jones' work revealed a streak of self-mocking humor that enabled him happily to don ridiculous disguises that could fool a villain but not the youngest kid in the audience.

William Boyd, who played Hopalong Cassidy, portrayed him as a super hero who never drank, cheated or thought unclean thoughts.

When Frances Smith grew up in Texas, her greatest dream was to some day marry Tom Mix and have six kids. Instead she married a man named Leonard Slye, but by then she had changed her name to Dale Evans, and he was known as Roy Rogers. Tom Mix was his hero too.

Tom Mix

One theme has remained steady, however, then and now: the cowboy that Louis L'Amour described as "a lone riding man in a lonesome country, riding toward a destiny of which he knows nothing, a man who had for years known no other life than this, nor wished for any other." In countless films — "The Westerner," "The Gunfighter," "Lonely are the Brave," the hero was a wanderer, sometimes willing to reveal his past, sometimes not, always ready to ride. Television's early heroes like Hopalong Cassidy and the Lone Ranger, and latter-day vagabonds like Palladin and Maverick and the Rawhide cowpunchers slept on new ground every night.

In the 1940s and 1950s, Western writers and directors succeeded in producing many of the genre's most enduring films, concerned with the hard conflicts imposed by the settlement of the West — ranchers battling farmers, and civilized towns fighting anarchistic outlaws. Shane, a vagabond gunslinger played by Alan Ladd, befriends homesteaders threatened by cattle barons.

In "High Noon," retiring marshal Will Cane, played ever so stoically by Gary Cooper, stands up to a gang of outlaws.

Gary Cooper came in to right things in "The Westerner," when Judge Roy Bean took the law "west of the Pecos" into his own hands.

In any of the films, the actual work of the cowboy was seldom brought up. "Red River," starring John Wayne and Montgomery Clift, is one of only a handful that examine the trail drive era. The only television series that treated cattle driving was "Rawhide," which ran for seven years.

When movies became "talkies" in the 1930s, the good ole standby Western suffered. Now relegated to B-movie status, it played in neighborhood theaters or as the second bill in the newly fashioned "double bill" (an innovation to bring depression-wise patrons into the theater). Even in its serial Saturday-movie form, it made money. But most were run up in less than two weeks. The Gene Autry and Roy Rogers "singing cowboy" films were shot in an amazing six days each.

Roy Rogers and Trigger

It wasn't just the cowboy who became a movie personality. His horse was a star too.

Trigger was the noblest of Hollywood's horses. Roy Rogers and Dale Evans were so devoted to him that when Trigger died they had the animal mounted and placed on display in their Apple Valley, California museum.

Buck Jones's horse Silver was so smart he could untie knots, bring Buck back to consciousness, and help him save the day.

And who could forget Gene Autry, bounding up over Champion's hind quarters and landing in the saddle just as the horse galloped off to chase the outlaws. Both the horse and rider are immortalized in the Gene Autry Museum in Los Angeles.

Gene Autry

The era of the B's stretched from the early 1930s to the late 1950s when television sounded their death knell. The picture that finally brought the Western back was "Stagecoach," first of a new Western genre that added a fresh element, the emphasis on character and mood. It brought in good actors in good vehicles — Gary Cooper in "High Noon," Alan Ladd as the regretful gunman in "Shane," Dana Andrews in "The Ox-Bow Incident," James Stewart's fine characterization in "Destry Rides Again."

Perhaps the biggest "special something" that producers offered in these movies was the stars themselves, none of whom were strictly western performers, but all of whom were solid box office draws regardless of the genre.

Few stars could outshine Kirk Douglas in "Lonely Are the Brave." He played a cowboy who escapes from jail and is hunted by a sheriff's posse, demonstrating the contrast between the old way of life and the modernization of today, with the cowboy as a man out of his time element.

John Wayne

Although the film portrayal of the American cowboy has only the slightest, most tenuous connection to the actual cowboy of the 1860s, it is perhaps the movie cowboy that seems most real to Americans. If asked "who is the cowboy?" most might answer John Wayne as the likely prototype. Or Tom Mix of their childhood years. Or even our "cowboy President," Ronald Reagan.

And who knows? Perhaps even the cowboy himself secretly likes to think of himself in a version of that role. Maybe there are moments when he sees himself as John Wayne.

While the Saturday cowboy matinees that enthralled kids in the 1930s may never have achieved adult critical acclaim, their place in history has been assured by the National Cowboy Hall of Fame's annual Western Heritage Awards, presented in a sort of Hollywood Oscar event. Stars from the fields of movies, television, music and literature don their best black tie attire for this gala celebration. Honors have been bestowed on hundreds of luminaries, including John Wayne, James Stewart, Clint Eastwood, John Ford, Louis L'Amour and James Michener.

During the 1930s there was no greater excitement for a ten-year-old boy than the Saturday-matinee Cowboy Serial at the local movie house. While the kids sat enthralled in the front-row seats, the cowboy hero leaped from the saloon roof onto his waiting horse and swept across the desert sands in pursuit of the fleeing outlaws. Every episode ended with a cliff-hanger. The hero was always left in a perilous situation — on a narrow rock on the edge of a cliff, with no rope, no help, and obviously (to the audience) no way out, with certain death thousands of feet below.

The next episode (to be continued) took place the following Saturday when the hordes of youngsters returned to find out what happened to Tom Mix or Buck Jones. After recapping the last episode, the rescue was revealed: the hero had dived into the lake below (not shown in the previous episode) and the adventure continued, gripping the audience to the point of an addiction that would bring them back to the next Saturday's showing.

In one of the most memorable of these episodic endings, the Bad Guys had Tom Mix cornered in a deep pit. When they opened a water flow, it became apparent that Tom Mix was in for it now; drowning was inevitable. The water rose higher and higher, and the hero was neck deep with no obvious way out when the screen posted its usual message: To Be Continued.

Did he drown? Never on Saturday afternoon. Next week the serial continued; the hero had stayed afloat with the rising water. When it hit ground level, he swam out.

The young audience was fascinated. The movie industry got rich.

KEEPING THE SPIRIT OF THE WEST ALIVE

High on Persimmon Hill above Oklahoma City, a unique segment of America's cowboy life is preserved in the National Cowboy Hall of Fame. The Hall is divided into several galleries representing various levels of the Western epoch.

First, there's the Old West of the epic trail drive, the vast roundups, the impromptu rodeos around the campfire. There's also the "imaginary" West of the film stars -- Roy Rogers, James Arness, John Wayne, Walter Brennan -- who almost seemed to transcend "imaginary" and become reality. The West of Today and Tomorrow is honored in another gallery, the Children's Cowboy Corral, where kids don chaps and boots and take to the trail for a first-hand taste of cowboy life, and perhaps a chance to be a trail boss.

But perhaps nothing in the Hall stirs the Western soul so much as the immense statue of Buffalo Bill on his rearing horse, his rifle pointed forever West -- the quintessential cowboy of Yesterday.

Spellbound youngsters gather around story-teller John Newman at the Institute of Texan Culture in San Antonio to hear the lore and legend of cowboy life in days when free-roaming longhorn cattle were everywhere in the south of Texas, and immense herds were driven from Texas ranges to Kansas cattle markets. Elsewhere in the Institute they'll see more aspects of Texas cowboy life.

Still Ridin' and Ropin'

Suddenly the frontier was chewed up. In the aftermath of the frontier's demise, there has been little left to do but wonder how it was – or surely must have been – to wish that we could have remained cowboys out in the open spaces. Yet a few do remain cowboys. They live with a kind of saddle-won self assurance, convinced that civilization is just whatever you happen to be up against.

At the peak of the cowboy era, it is estimated some 40,000 men made a living working cattle. Now there aren't half that many. It's a job that not everybody is able — or crazy enough — to do. The hours are long, the pay is meager.

But he doesn't need much, he says. He owns his horse and he owns the saddle. He can always up and quit, maybe head for Idaho. In fact, Idaho was nice, he recalls.

The cowboy is a skilled practitioner of his craft, often suffering isolation — like the first cowboys. But there are still a few of them around. They can be found in places like Twin Bridges, Montana and Tuscarora, Nevada, in Alpine, Texas and Anadarko, Oklahoma.

For Eric DeWitt, a 34-year-old cowboy in Arizona's rugged Santa Catalina mountains, the cowboy life is what he has chosen. He likes solitude and the challenge of relying on his own skills in a landscape so tough to traverse that a helping hand is seventeen miles away on a dirt road.

He doesn't see that cowboy life has changed much in a hundred years. His day starts at sunrise, heading out on his horse to cover 100 square miles of rocks and cactus. He's got a truck, but it's pure hell to lumber along in low gear pitching over washboard dirt and solid rocks. It's not so bad traveling east/west, because that's the direction the canyons take. He can ride the bottom, or trot along the ridge. If he has to travel north, it's a day's ride for sure, crossing canyons.

He never runs out of things to do, from shoeing horses to riding fence. His brother Douglas helps him at roundup. For branding he uses a small "running iron" that he packs in his saddlebag.

He admits it's no easy job. "But if it's the lifestyle you want, you cut a deal," he says. "Whatever happens, I know I'm going to have a job, and I know I'm going to be a cowboy."

The 21-year-old Wyoming cowhand admits "we're underpaid, overworked. . .I haven't been to town in two months," then quickly adds, "I wouldn't trade this life for any other on a bet."

Today's cowboy may do part of his work with pickup truck and jeep, even helicopter. But he still spends long hours in the saddle in harsh weather, searching the vastness for steers.

The ZX ranch near Paisley, Oregon is so big it takes all day in a four-wheel drive to see just a piece of it. Sometimes there are 4,500 cows in a single field. The country is desolate, wide open. Once, when a vandal shot holes in the water tank, all the wild horses in the area died of dehydration.

Ranch manager Bob deBraga says before he was a teen he knew what his future would be. Like John Wayne, he speaks in low gear, with care, very slowly. "I wanted to be around buckaroos, have cows, see a lot of country." He worked first in northeast Nevada, "learned to cope with just about anything Mother Nature can throw; ten feet of snow in California high country, winds that can rip the hide off, heat that can melt a mountain." He and his wife, together, earned $200 a month.

He chuckles when young cowboys talk about going back to the good old days. "I've been there," he says, "with my ol' bedroll, following a wagon around. When it rains, everything you own is soaking wet. You don't get a shower till you fall in the crick."

o

Yet in spite of a life of bone-weariness and loneliness, of punishing work and living with ornery cows, cowboys do live to be old men.

Waltzy Elliot, at the age of 87, could look back on a long, full life as a cowpuncher. By the time he was twelve, he recalls, he was driving wagons and breaking horses for saddle. "Cowboying was a dollar a day, but you got three good meals along with it."

He remembers the miserable freezing winters of 1924 and 1925 in Winnemucca, Nevada, loading cattle all day. But he also remembers days of play and dancing. "In those days," he says, "dancing was really something. Why, you started in the evening and you'd have a midnight supper and dance until sun-up."

It's not an easy life. But the cowboy is that rare creature in an over-civilized world. He's his own man.

The outdoors is his. Alone on his horse, he's known sunrise in Idaho, the mist rising up from the meadows. He's marvelled at the wide prairie stretching to the horizon and a herd of cattle almost too numerous to see across. He's lived through winter snows and seen the first greening of spring. He's heard the lonesome howl of the coyote while cooking coffee and beans over an open campfire. In a line shack in the Sierra he's lived among the tall pines, watched shadows falling across his shack from the highest peaks.

If you're looking for him, you'll find him on a horse somewhere out on the rangelands of Idaho or Colorado, or riding fence in Wyoming, or maybe downing a beer in a Nevada saloon. He's easy to spot because he looks like a cowboy ought to look. His skin has the texture of beef jerky, his scuffed boots are sharp-toed, his jeans ride low on his waist, the stubby remains of a Bull Durham cigarette dangle from his lips. There is a bit of a stoop in his stance and an easy grace in the way he mounts a horse. He's as real as the sweat stains on his battered old Stetson.

o

Asked if he liked his job, one cowpuncher snorted, "You call this a job? It's the sorriest damn line of work I ever heard of. Long hours, low pay. You want to know why I punch cows? It's because I love every mortal minute of it!"

The Weather-Worn Cowman

"When your joints are cold and stiff, and an old pony is doing his double best to unload you, a cowboy don't feel none too happy," said the Nevada buckaroo. "Some fall morning you wake up to four inches of wet snow on your bed tarp. If you got your feet wet yesterday, it's pure hell to pull those cold damp boots on. Even so, there's a certain glamour that clings to a cowboy. You remember riding the deep canyon of the Owyhee, the bands of wild horses, the sagebrush flats and rugged mountains of Nevada. And when you look back over all the years, remembering the horses, cattle, girls, and the men you rode with, you kinda know the good outweighed the bad."